Primary Sources of the Abolitionist Movement

Harriet Tubman and the Underground Railroad

Susan Dudley Gold

New York

Published in 2016 by Cavendish Square Publishing, LLC
243 5th Avenue, Suite 136, New York, NY 10016

Copyright © 2016 by Cavendish Square Publishing, LLC

First Edition

Library of Congress Cataloging-in-Publication Data

Gold, Susan Dudley.
Harriet Tubman and the Underground Railroad / Susan Dudley Gold.
pages cm. — (Primary sources of the abolitionist movement)
Includes bibliographical references and index.
ISBN 978-1-50260-522-1 (hardcover) ISBN 978-1-50260-523-8 (ebook)
1. Tubman, Harriet, 1820?-1913—Juvenile literature. 2. Slaves—United States—Biography—Juvenile literature.
3. African American women—Biography—Juvenile literature. 4. Underground Railroad—Juvenile literature.
I. Title.

E444.T82G65 2015
326'.8092—dc23
[B]

2015002016

Editorial Director: David McNamara
Editor: Amy Hayes
Copy Editor: Cynthia Roby
Art Director: Jeffrey Talbot
Senior Designer: Amy Greenan
Senior Production Manager: Jennifer Ryder-Talbot
Production Editor: Renni Johnson
Photo Researcher: J8 Media

CONTENTS

Slavery and Abolition

In 1776, the thirteen colonies of the British Empire formed a new nation in North America. In declaring their independence, the leaders of the American Revolution stated their belief "that all men are created equal, that they are endowed by their Creator with certain unalienable Rights, that among these are Life, Liberty and the pursuit of Happiness." The Declaration of Independence did not apply to America's slaves, however. Many of the new nation's leaders publically said they hated slavery. President George Washington called it "repugnant." Thomas Jefferson described slavery as "a hideous blot" on the United States. Yet both Washington and Jefferson owned slaves themselves.

The early founders believed that the nation's economy would fail if slavery were abolished. Southern landowners had millions of dollars invested in slaves. Their crops,

Southern plantation owners relied on slaves to harvest their cotton crops. This woodcut shows the hard physical labor slaves had to endure.

tobacco and cotton, fueled the economy. Northern mills relied on the cotton harvested by slaves to produce clothing and other textiles. Shipping firms, banks, and import/export companies based in northern states also benefited from the cotton trade. Southern planters exported raw cotton to England and other foreign ports. This brought wealth to the country and valuable, needed goods in exchange for cotton. By the mid-1800s, the American South produced two-thirds of the world's cotton.

Southern leaders argued that each state should be able to determine its own rules and laws. They claimed the right to decide whether or not to allow slavery within their states' borders. People in other states, they said, should have no say in that decision.

Not everyone believed that slavery could be justified by economics or states' rights. Even before the American Revolution, Quakers and other religious leaders spoke out against slavery. They saw the hypocrisy of basing a new nation on equality and freedom while allowing part of the population to be enslaved. The abolitionists—those seeking to abolish or end slavery—believed it was morally wrong to enslave human beings. They pushed to outlaw slavery in America and elsewhere.

By 1819, all blacks in Canada had been declared free residents. The British Parliament voted in 1833 to end slavery in the British colonies. Mexico put limits on slavery in 1820 and abolished it nine years later. Slavery had been officially barred in the North by 1830.

Some abolitionists worked against slavery by helping runaway slaves escape. Many fugitives traveled a secret network of safe houses and hidden pathways, known as the **Underground Railroad**, to freedom. Few slaves made it to safety. Some, with nowhere to go, returned after days or weeks of hiding nearby. Bloodhounds quickly tracked down others. Slave owners posted notices offering rewards for missing slaves. **Slave catchers**, attracted by the rewards, scoured the area for fugitives. Landowners formed slave patrols to keep watch for runaway slaves. All slaves were required to carry passes signed by their owners whenever they traveled off the **plantations**.

Slaves who tried to escape and failed endured savage beatings. Some were **lynched**, or hanged, by angry slave owners to set an example for other slaves wanting to be free.

Into this world of violence and fear, Harriet Tubman was born around the year 1822.

CHAPTER ONE

Life As a Slave

I magine being born into slavery. You live in a drafty wood cabin, are given little to eat, and dress in ragged clothes. You are a young child being forced to pick cotton in sunbaked fields ten or more hours each day. If you complain or take a break, an overseer will beat you with a whip. You may be sent away from your mother to work for a stranger on another plantation. Imagine that your father and brother no longer live with you. They were sold to a trader and taken to a plantation far away. You will never see them again.

This is only a glimpse into the world in which Southern slaves existed during the early 1800s.

America's first slaves came from Africa. Beginning as early as the 1500s, African slave traders captured men, women, and children and sold them to Europeans.

Slave quarters on a plantation in the South in the mid-1800s. Many slaves grew their own vegetables in gardens near their cabins to supplement their meager diet.

The European traders transported the captives to the Americas. From the 1500s to the 1800s, at least twelve million Africans were seized and carried to the New World. Most landed in South America and the islands of the Caribbean. Almost half a million were brought to North America. The first shipload of slaves in America joined English settlers in Jamestown, Virginia, in 1619.

During the monthlong journey across the sea, thousands died. Those who survived were herded like cattle to the town square and sold to the highest bidder. The buyers separated parents from children. Siblings were sold to different landowners and never saw one another again. They spent the rest of their lives in captivity, forced to labor for other men's gain. Their children and their children's children faced the same grim future.

Harriet Tubman and the Underground Railroad

Armed slave traders captured entire African families and shipped them to the Americas to be sold as slaves. The men, women, and children in this illustration have been shackled and are being taken from their homes.

Tubman's Early Childhood

In 1820, slightly more than 1.5 million slaves lived in the United States. Though some slaves lived in the North, most resided in the South, where they worked on plantations, toiled on small farms, or performed household chores. Southern planters depended on slaves to tend their tobacco and cotton crops. White landowners considered slaves inferior beings. They believed it was

Harriet Tubman carried a small pistol with her on her trips along the freedom trail. She carried a rifle like the one pictured here during her Civil War service.

their right to own them and use their labor without paying them. The landowners treated slaves as property, to buy or sell as needed. Slaves had no rights—not even the right to life. A landowner could beat a slave to death without penalty.

States did not record the births of slaves, so Harriet Tubman was never sure of her exact age or birthdate. Most sources, however, state her birth year as 1822. She was born on Maryland's eastern shore, on a plantation owned by Anthony Thompson. Her parents, Harriet (also known as Rit) Green and Ben Ross, named her Araminta. Family members called her "Minty." She would change her name to Harriet after she escaped slavery.

Harriet was fifth of nine children. One of her earliest memories was being tossed playfully into the air by two young white women who lived in the house of the **master**. Harriet learned soon enough that life as a slave would not be fun and games. When Harriet was still a toddler, Edward Brodess, Thompson's stepson, took Harriet's mother and her children, including little Minty, to his farm. Harriet lived in slave quarters on the Brodess estate with her mother and brothers and sisters. Her father had to stay behind and work on the nearby Thompson plantation.

As a young man, Brodess struggled with his small farm. To raise money, he sold two of Harriet's older sisters. Years later, Harriet would still remember the look of agony on her sisters' faces and their cries as the new owners dragged them away to labor on a chain gang in Georgia. One sister was forced to leave behind her baby. Harriet's mother looked on in "hopeless grief," knowing she would never see her daughters again.

At age five, Harriet had to leave her home to work for a family who rented her from Brodess. Slave owners often rented out slaves when they did not need them on their own plantations. The rent money was paid to the owner. Harriet's new mistress, Miss Susan, a married woman who lived nearby, proved to be a cruel taskmaster.

Harriet, not much bigger than a toddler, was expected to clean the house and care for a baby. She had never been trained as a housemaid and had no idea how to do household chores. When she swept the dust from the floor, it settled on the furniture. This made it seem as if she had not done her chores. Her enraged mistress, Miss Susan, whipped Harriet severely. The mistress's sister showed the frightened girl what to do.

Harriet, small for her age, could not carry the baby and had to sit down and hold it in her lap. After a full day's work, she had to sleep by the baby's crib and keep it from crying. If the baby woke in the night and made a noise, Miss Susan grabbed her whip and beat Harriet. She bore those marks on her neck and shoulders for the rest of her life.

At about age six or seven, Harriet went to a local farm owned by James Cook and his wife. From the start, the Cooks worked Harriet almost beyond endurance. She had to check on muskrat traps that were set in cold swamp water. The job taught her how to survive in the wilderness—skills she would make good use of later in her efforts to free slaves.

The work continued even when Harriet became ill with the measles. Finally, she became so sick that the Cooks returned her to her owner. She left the Cooks' farm marked with scars from their abuse.

Harsh Conditions

The harsh treatment Tubman faced was not unusual in America's South. Slaves endured long, hard days in the fields. Many times, they had to survive on scraps of food and vegetables they raised in gardens near their quarters— if their master allowed it. After the workday was over, they tended the gardens at night. Mary Reynolds, who was born a slave in Louisiana in the 1830s, said her master provided "only a half barrel [of] water," which was "stale and hot," for the workers in the field. "Mostly we ate pickled pork and corn bread and peas and beans and 'taters. [There] never was as much as we needed."

Slave children wore ragged clothes discarded by the master's children. They had no underwear, no coats, and

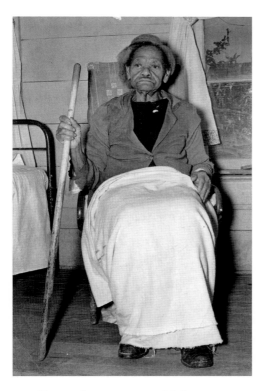

ill-fitting shoes or none at all. Cabins had beds made of wood planks laid across poles. Mattresses were filled with corncobs. Children often slept on the floor of the slave cabins or outside the bedroom of the white person they served.

Punishment could be extreme and brutal, depending on the master and the offense. Mary Reynolds said in her slave narrative:

> I seed them put the men and women in the stock with [their] hands screwed down through holes in the board and [their] feet tied together and [their] naked behinds to the world. Solomon the overseer beat them … cut the flesh most to the bones …

When Harriet Tubman was twelve years old, she tried to help another slave and almost paid with her life. She worked as a field hand and saw another slave slip away without permission. She followed him to the

Bucktown Village Store to warn him that the overseer was on his way to punish him. When the overseer arrived, he ordered Harriet to tie up the runaway. She refused, and the other slave fled. Furious, the overseer hurled a two-pound iron bar at the fleeing slave. The bar missed the slave but hit Harriet squarely in the head. It knocked her unconscious, and she almost died. Headaches and seizures tormented her for the rest of her life. She would fall asleep without warning and remain in a trancelike state for some time. Harriet had vivid dreams and saw visions, which she interpreted as being signs from God. Deeply religious, Harriet relied on her faith in God to protect her and guide her through difficult and dangerous times.

Brodess tried to sell Harriet, but because of her injury no one would buy her. Instead, Brodess rented her out. As a teen, Harriet spent much of her time in the woods, cutting and hauling logs for the Stewart family. She also drove oxen, plowed, lifted heavy barrels filled with goods, and carried grain to the family's mill. The physical labor left Harriet strong and well prepared for outdoor living. She became familiar with the waterways and the black seamen who ferried timber along the rivers. Like most slaves, Harriet never learned to read or write. In some states, it was against the law to teach slaves reading and writing. But Harriet became an expert on the natural world around her.

When Anthony Thompson died, he freed Harriet's father, Ben Ross, in his will. Ross was also given a plot of land on the Thompson plantation, where he had a cabin. Ross worked for the Stewarts harvesting timber. He connected Harriet to the network of free blacks who lived and worked in the area. Many were former slaves.

Harriet's mother, Rit, was supposed to be freed when she reached age forty-five, according to her original master's will. Instead, she remained enslaved by the Brodesses for years. Ben eventually paid Eliza Brodess (Edward's widow) twenty dollars for ownership rights to Rit.

When Harriet was about twenty-two, she married John Tubman, who had been born a free man. He lived near Harriet's father in a small community of free blacks west of the Brodess farm. Harriet had to get permission from Brodess to marry John. Despite her marriage, she remained a slave. The young couple probably lived together at least part of the time in the free black community. Brodess agreed to let Harriet work for various masters. He received fifty or sixty dollars a year for her services. Tubman was allowed to keep any additional pay she earned. With this money, she bought a pair of oxen and hauled timber and other loads for pay.

Even with this arrangement, Harriet remained the property of Brodess. When he died in March 1849, Brodess's widow began selling slaves to pay off the estate's debts. Harriet's niece and her young child were sold to a local businessman. The threat of further sales loomed over the family. They feared other relatives would be sold to faraway buyers. Rather than being shipped to a distant plantation, Harriet decided to run away. Her husband, a free man, tried to talk her out of her plan. He refused to join her on such a dangerous journey.

THREE HUNDRED DOLLARS REWARD.

RANAWAY from the subscriber on Monday the 17th ult., three negroes, named as follows: HARRY, aged about 19 years, has on one side of his neck a won, just under the ear, he is of a dark chestnut color, about 5 feet 8 or 9 inches hight; BEN, aged about 25 years, is very quick to speak when spoken to, he is of a chestnut color, about six feet high; MINTY, aged about 27 years, is of a chestnut color, fine looking, and about 5 feet high. One hundred dollars reward will be given for each of the above named negroes, if taken out of the State, and $50 each if taken in the State. They must be lodged in Baltimore, Easton or Cambridge Jail, in Maryland.

ELIZA ANN BRODESS.
Near Bucktown, Dorchester county, Md.
Oct. 3d, 1849.

☞ The Delaware Gazette will please copy the above three weeks, and charge this office.

Eliza Brodess offered a $300 reward for the return of Harriet Tubman and her two brothers in this advertisement published in the *Cambridge Democrat* in 1849. Tubman's brothers returned to the plantation on their own, forcing Harriet to accompany them.

On September 17, 1849, Harriet and two of her brothers ran away and headed for freedom. The widow Brodess offered a three-hundred-dollar reward for their return. The poster described Harry (Henry) as nineteen with a mole on his neck and of "dark chestnut color." Ben, about twenty-five, was said to be "very quick to speak" and about six feet tall. Minty (Harriet), about twenty-seven, was "fine looking, and about 5 feet high."

The trio did not get far before the two brothers decided to return to the plantation. They feared what would happen to them if they were caught. Despite Harriet's pleas, they dragged her back with them.

The following month, Harriet set out alone. She was determined to be free.

Gone But Not Forgotten

Former slave John W. Fields, at age eighty-nine

Slaves lived in fear that their children or other loved ones would be taken away from them. For many, that nightmare came true.

John W. Fields was born a slave in Kentucky in 1848. Like Harriet Tubman, he came from a large family, with eleven brothers and sisters. Fields was six when his master died, and the slaves were divided among the heirs.

We slaves were divided by this method. Three disinterested persons were chosen to come to the plantation and together they wrote the names of the different heirs on a few slips of paper. These slips were put in a hat and passed among us slaves. Each one took a slip and the name of the slip was the new owner ... I can't describe the heartbreak and horror of that separation. I was only six years old, and it was the last time I ever saw my mother for longer than one night.

His mother could visit her children one week each year, but she had to divide her time among different plantations and could stay for only a brief time with each one. Other slave parents, like Harriet Tubman's family, never saw their children again after they were sold to new owners.

Going Underground

English abolitionist and reformer William Wilberforce. Around 1790, he helped end the international slave trade as a member of Parliament.

A growing number of abolitionists worked on both sides of the Atlantic to end slavery. A major triumph was scored when they ended the international **slave trade** between Africa and the Americas. Under the leadership of abolitionist William Wilberforce, the British Parliament passed the Abolition of the Slave Trade Act in 1807. A year later, on January 1, 1808, the United States banned the international slave trade. By the 1830s, the slave trade was illegal worldwide.

Abolitionists help a group of fugitive slaves escape to freedom along the Underground Railroad.

The end of the slave trade meant American slave owners had to rely on the slaves already in the United States and their offspring. Existing slaves became more valuable. When crops failed, landowners sold slaves to pay off debts or moved their operation to new lands farther south and west. These new farms relied on the labor of slaves from established plantations in the South. Some owners of the old plantations found it more profitable to buy and sell slaves rather than continue farming. Slave labor became so valuable that corrupt slave dealers kidnapped free blacks and sold them as slaves.

Sold South

The fear of being sold or moved to the Deep South spurred many slaves, including Tubman, to run away. Freedom was a powerful lure. However, huge roadblocks awaited slaves who tried to run to freedom. Because slaves were worth a lot of money, landowners did whatever they could to retrieve runaways. They posted notices offering rewards, sometimes as much as one thousand dollars or more, for especially good workers. The promise of riches attracted slave catchers, who specialized in capturing runaways. As in the poster shown describing George, Noah, and other runaways, notices gave detailed descriptions of fugitives.

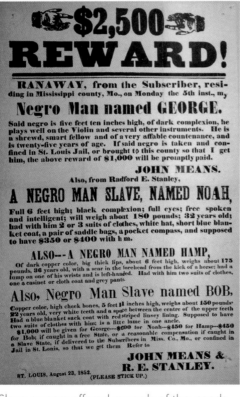

Slave owners offered rewards of thousands of dollars for runaway slaves, as seen in this poster from 1852.

Masters gave vicious beatings to runaway slaves and to anyone suspected of helping them or even knowing about a planned escape. Most slaves who tried to run away were caught. Bloodhounds, slave catchers, and patrols who demanded passes of every black person found off plantation grounds blocked the way to freedom. Slaves had little or no money and few provisions.

Mary Reynolds recalled a runaway who was chased down by hounds. The dogs pulled her out of a tree, ripped off her clothes, and attacked her. As a child, Reynolds worked with another slave named Turner. When Turner ran away, the master accused Mary of being in on the plans. The master stripped Mary, tied her to a tree, and beat her unconscious. She survived but was never able to have children as a result of the beating.

Walter Rimm, age eighty, recalls how his family helped a fellow slave, who escaped to freedom in Mexico.

Former slave Walter Rimm said his father tried to run away several times. The master whipped him every time he was caught.

Runaways used all kinds of tricks and methods to escape. Rimm knew a woman who put pepper in her socks to keep the hounds from tracking her. The pepper made the dogs sneeze. In 1849 Henry Brown, a slave on a Virginia plantation, made it to freedom when he hid in a box and shipped himself 350 miles (563.3 kilometers) to Philadelphia. The 5-foot-8-inch (1.73 meters) **freedom seeker** became known as Henry "Box" Brown.

Even with the threat of harsh punishment, slaves helped runaways as best they could. Rimm's mother fed a runaway slave who stopped by their cabin on his way to Mexico. Through the years, slaves and free blacks developed secret ways to communicate with each other and established informal routes of travel among their communities and to the wider world. Slaves followed these routes to visit family members on other plantations. Sometimes they used them to escape, either south to Mexico or North to **free states**.

A New Kind of Railroad

Opposition to slavery grew. The number of free states—those that banned slavery—increased. Black and white abolitionists in the North and the South developed a system, based on the informal routes, to aid fugitive slaves.

Sometime in the early 1830s the escape routes came to be known as the Underground Railroad. At that time steam locomotives had just begun carrying passengers along eastern railroads. The term Underground Railroad referred to the complex routes followed by those seeking freedom, as they seemed to vanish underground.

People adopted railroad terms to refer to the escape system. Safe houses, barns, caves, and other hiding places became known as **stations**. The men and women who operated the stations were called **stationmasters**. They provided food and supplies and directed fugitives to the next safe stop along the way. **Agents** helped by providing information and linking slaves to the underground system. **Conductors**, such as Harriet Tubman, led slaves along the route to freedom. All participants in the Underground Railroad risked their property and sometimes their lives by aiding runaway slaves. The conductors were particularly at risk. They met with slaves in the South and stayed with them on the arduous journey to freedom.

A white abolitionist conductor named Seth Concklin was among those who died trying to help fugitives. After several successes, Concklin failed in his attempt to rescue a slave family in Alabama (later known as the Stills). His friend N. R. Johnston wrote of his capture:

> And poor Concklin! I feel for him. When he is dragged back to Alabama, I fear they will go far beyond the utmost rigor of the law, and vent their savage cruelty upon him.

Unfortunately, Johnston's fears came true. Concklin was found in chains by a river, drowned, and with a fractured skull. Peter Still, who had fled to freedom earlier, eventually raised enough money to buy his family's freedom. His brother, William Still, lived in Philadelphia and was a leader in the abolition movement and a director of the Underground Railroad system. He helped hundreds of runaways and recorded the stories of almost seven hundred of them. Harriet Tubman often stopped at his office with her bands of freedom seekers.

By the time Harriet Tubman began her journey to freedom in October 1849, many slaves had escaped south to Mexico or north to free states. Newspapers often ran ads seeking runaway slaves and offering rewards. The census of 1850 recorded 259 fugitive slaves in Maryland, the most in any Southern state. The total number of runaways for the Southern states was listed as more than one thousand. There were probably many more slaves who tried and failed to escape. In addition, owners may not have admitted to census takers the full number of fugitives.

A secret communication network connected slaves, fugitives, free blacks, and their abolitionist supporters. They passed vital information by talking in code and singing hymns and other songs that held secret meaning. They exchanged information along the road or at chance meetings and whispered secrets to family members during visits. Those who could read and write sent coded letters to leaders in the network. In this way, free blacks, Quaker abolitionists and other white sympathizers, and slaves stood ready to help those who wanted to attempt the race to freedom.

Once Tubman made the decision to try another escape, she kept her plans secret. To maintain secrecy, fugitives did not reveal their route—before or after the journey. Fugitives often knew only the location of their first stop. At each station, they received directions to the next safe house. The route changed, as needed, to avoid slave patrols and other dangers that appeared.

Escape!

That October night in 1849, Tubman walked away from the plantation using the North Star to guide her. Just before daybreak, she stopped at the home of Maryland abolitionists. The white woman who lived there told her to grab a broom and sweep leaves in the yard. That way, if anyone passed by, they would think she was a slave performing her duties.

Tubman ate and rested during the day. Once night fell, she climbed aboard a wagon. To keep her hidden, the owner piled his load on top of her and drove to the next safe house. She moved from safe house to safe

An illustration of Harriet Tubman as she led fugitive slaves along the Underground Railroad. Tubman made at least thirteen trips along the secret route to rescue slaves in the South.

house, over and over. She may have stopped in Baltimore, where friends and relatives lived. After days of living in fear and nights of walking through swamps, forests, and fields, Tubman crossed the Maryland border into Pennsylvania—and freedom. During her ordeal, she covered more than one hundred miles. She later told her biographer, Sarah H. Bradford, of her joy at that moment.

> When I found I had crossed that line,
> I looked at my hands to see if I was the
> same person. There was such a glory over
> everything; the sun came like gold through
> the trees, and over the fields, and I felt like I
> was in Heaven.

Tubman settled in Philadelphia amid a community of white and black abolitionists. There she met prominent leaders of the **abolitionist movement**: Lucretia and James Mott, William Still, and others. They introduced her to the famed Boston abolitionist William Lloyd Garrison, black reformer Frederick Douglass, and William Seward, a US senator from Auburn, New York. Seward, a two-term governor of New York, became Abraham Lincoln's secretary of state in 1861.

As much as Tubman enjoyed being free, she missed her family. "There was no one to welcome me to the land of freedom, I was a stranger in a strange land; and my home, after all, was down in Maryland," she told Bradford. She wanted her family to be free, too. Word soon traveled to her that her niece Kessiah was about to be sold. Kessiah was only an infant when her mother, Tubman's older sister, had been sold to work on a Georgia chain gang years before. Kessiah was now a young woman, married to a free black man with two young children of her own.

When Tubman heard this disturbing news in December 1850, she contacted Kessiah's husband, John Bowley, through the secret communications network. Together they devised a plot to rescue Kessiah and her children. On the day of the auction, a crowd of slave traders gathered on the steps of the courthouse in Cambridge, Maryland. During a break in the auction, Bowley managed to smuggle his wife and children away to a safe house close to the courthouse. Bowley, an experienced sailor, then led his family to a small boat and headed out on a dangerous journey along Chesapeake Bay.

Tubman met them when they arrived, cold and wet, in Baltimore. She too was in great danger as a fugitive slave. If anyone had recognized her or found her actions

Slave traders auctioned off enslaved African Americans in town squares throughout the South. In this illustration, a prospective buyer examines a slave before he places a bid.

suspicious, she could have been quickly captured and returned to the Eastern Shore. After hiding with friends, the group followed Tubman to safety in Philadelphia.

Later that spring Tubman led her brother Moses and two of his friends to Pennsylvania after they escaped to Baltimore.

By the fall of 1851, Tubman had been free for two years. She longed to live with her husband, John Tubman. Risking everything, she returned to Dorchester County—where her former master lived and where she was well known—and set out to bring her husband to the North. When she arrived, she discovered that John Tubman did not want to go north with her. He had given up on their relationship and married a free black woman named Caroline.

The news crushed Tubman. She loved her husband and his betrayal angered her. However, she soon realized that she could live without him. Others in the area needed and wanted her help. She left with a group of fugitives and steered them safely along the Underground Railroad to Philadelphia.

Thirteen Trips

Over the next nine years, Harriet Tubman continued her journeys back to Maryland to bring other members of her family and friends to freedom. In all, she made about thirteen trips to the South and rescued around seventy people from slavery. In addition to those Tubman rescued personally, many other fugitives followed her instructions to Underground Railroad stops and made their own treacherous journeys to freedom.

Each trip Tubman made back to Maryland put her at risk. Slave catchers roamed the territory looking for runaways. Slaveholders and slaves in the area knew Tubman. Word spread that she would lead people to freedom, and they kept a sharp eye out. Tubman and the freedom seekers had many narrow escapes.

The home of Thomas Garrett in Wilmington, Delaware, became one of Tubman's frequent stops on the Underground Railroad. Garrett, a Quaker, ran a hardware store and helped more than two thousand slaves to freedom. Garrett twice went to trial for aiding fugitive slaves. The fines, amounting to thousands of dollars, ruined him financially. At the end of one trial, he told the judge: "I haven't a dollar of property in the world, but if thee knows a fugitive that needs a breakfast this morning, send him to me."

Tubman made most of her trips to Maryland during the winter months. At that time of year, nights were longer, giving those seeking freedom more hours to travel in darkness. At times a terrified, exhausted fugitive might decide the road to freedom was too difficult and refuse to continue. That threatened the entire operation. Slave owners could force the would-be runaway to betray the rest of the group. In answer, Tubman would pull a pistol from under her skirt and point it at the rebel. "You go on or die!" she would warn. That got the fugitive back on his feet. She never left a freedom seeker behind, and she never had to fire the pistol.

Tubman arranged to meet freedom seekers at a slave cabin or other sites. The groups traveled by night, climbing mountains, crossing rivers, crawling through swamps, and passing through woods and fields. Tubman brought along medicine that would make babies drowsy so their cries would not alert slave catchers. On more than one occasion, slave catchers passed within feet of Tubman and her band as they hid in holes or behind trees. Tubman sometimes left a group in hiding while she scouted the area. On her return, she signaled the group by singing a hymn. "Go down, Moses," sung in a clear, happy tone, told the fugitives they were safe. By changing the words or picking up the pace, Tubman told the group whether they should come quickly or continue hiding until the danger passed.

In between trips to Maryland, Tubman rented a room in Philadelphia and worked as a cook and housekeeper for hotels and private homes. She saved the money she earned to help finance her freedom runs to rescue her family and others. Abolitionist groups in the United States and in England, as well as individuals such as Thomas Garrett and Lucretia Mott, also contributed to the effort.

Harriet Tubman poses with neighbors and family in a photo taken around 1885 in Auburn, New York. *From left to right*: Harriet Tubman; Gertie Davis, her adopted daughter; Nelson Davis, Harriet's husband; Lee Chaney; John Alexander; Walter Green; and Sarah Parker.

Master of Disguise

Tubman became skilled at hiding in plain sight when she returned to Maryland, where she was wanted as a fugitive slave. Often she posed as an elderly black woman or man. She wore a bonnet or hat pulled down to hide her face and bent over when she walked.

On one trip to Dorchester County, Tubman saw her former master standing nearby. She quickly grabbed a newspaper and pretended to be reading it. The master, knowing that Tubman could not read, never suspected that the old black woman browsing the paper was his fugitive slave.

As added security, Tubman sometimes carried a live chicken or two. If she met a slave catcher or someone who might recognize her, she released the chickens, causing a flap. The would-be capturers, distracted by the chickens, paid no attention to the old slave chasing them.

Tubman used similar techniques to blend in when she spied for the **Union** Army during the Civil War. By posing as slaves, she and the black soldiers who accompanied her were able to obtain valuable information for the army.

Harriet Tubman and the Underground Railroad

CHAPTER THREE

Fugitive Slave Laws and Escape to Canada

Enslaved blacks had tried to run away from their masters since the first ships delivered slaves to America's shores. When the new nation formed after the American Revolution, Southerners demanded that the Constitution include a provision requiring other states to return their fugitive slaves. Article IV, Section 2 gave slaveholders the right to reclaim slaves who had escaped to states where slavery was banned.

> No Person held to Service or Labour in one State, under the Laws thereof, escaping into another, shall, in Consequence of any Law or Regulation therein, be discharged from such

Slave catchers capture a runaway slave under fugitive slave laws in effect at the time.

Service or Labour, but shall be delivered up
on Claim of the Party to whom such Service
or Labour may be due.

The provision remained as part of the Constitution until the passage of Thirteenth Amendment barred slavery throughout the nation in 1865.

Even with Article IV in place, Southern landowners pushed for a law to ensure the return of their slaves. The second Congress passed a fugitive slave act in January 1793. Josiah Parker of Virginia, one of only two Southerners in the House to vote against the bill, was a Quaker who referred to himself as a reluctant slave owner. Although some Quakers owned slaves, most of the religion's followers opposed slavery. President George

Although the US Constitution did not mention slavery directly, Article IV gave slaveholders the right to reclaim fugitive slaves—those "held to service or labour" who escaped into free states.

Washington signed the bill into law on February 12, 1793. The new law set a fine of five hundred dollars for anyone who took steps to "obstruct or hinder" a person who was retrieving a suspected fugitive.

Beginning in 1816, a group of slaveholders and white abolitionists formed the American Colonization Society and began efforts to transport American blacks to Liberia, where they could live in freedom. Slaveholders supported the relocation of free blacks, whom they feared would inspire their slaves to run away. Some abolitionists joined the effort because they believed the nation's white society would never allow blacks to live in America as equals. The American Colonization Society eventually relocated about twelve thousand black Americans to Liberia.

Many abolitionists, black and white, opposed the colonization movement. Most American blacks had no desire to live in Africa. They considered America their homeland. Like Harriet Tubman, they focused on attaining freedom for slaves in their own country.

Several northern states had laws that required the return of fugitive slaves to their owners. However, as time passed and more northern states banned slavery, opposition to fugitive slave laws grew in the North. It became clear that the slavery question still separated

North and South when Missouri sought to become a state. Slaveholders in Missouri wanted Congress to allow slavery in the new state. Abolitionists rejected Missouri's bid to enter the nation as a **slave state**. The Missouri Compromise, which Congress approved in 1820, created two new states: Missouri, where slavery was allowed, and Maine, an antislavery state. It also divided the nation into a southern region, where slavery would be permitted, and northern areas, where slavery would be banned. As part of the deal, the compromise included a new fugitive slave act that required the return of slaves who escaped into free territory. The compromise enraged abolitionists. They became even more determined to end slavery.

Scandals and horror stories from escaped slaves about their treatment strengthened the abolition movement. Federal law allowed slave catchers and others to seize fugitives who had escaped to free states. The law did not require approval from northern courts or officials.

Solomon Northup around 1853

Unscrupulous slave catchers used the loose terms of the law to snatch free blacks who lived in the North and sell them into slavery in the South. One such case involved Solomon Northup, a free black man who was kidnapped in 1841 and taken to Louisiana. He spent the next twelve years enslaved on a plantation until northern friends won his freedom. Northup's book, *Twelve Years a Slave*, detailed the abuse he suffered at the hands of Southern slaveholders.

Even Northerners who took no stand on slavery objected to laws that allowed Southerners to override their system of justice and seize black residents without trial or court ruling. Pennsylvania, among others, passed a series of laws that challenged the federal fugitive slave act. Under one provision, anyone who seized a runaway without a warrant could be charged as a kidnapper. Several states in the North passed personal liberty laws that guaranteed fugitive slaves certain legal rights. Some states required that fugitive slaves be allowed a jury trial before their return to a slaveholder. Northern states even passed laws forbidding state officials from aiding in the return of slaves. Such laws did not prevent the return of slaves whose owners provided the required proof of ownership. They did delay the process, however, and made it "expensive and annoying" for owners, according to one Massachusetts newspaper.

Southerners railed against these laws and the continuing activities of Harriet Tubman and others who used the Underground Railroad to free slaves. They were determined to stop the loss of what they considered their property. They demanded that Congress take further action to protect their assets.

In 1848, the year before Tubman escaped to the North, the United States defeated Mexico and acquired a huge chunk of land that would become the states of Arizona, New Mexico, and California, as well as parts of Nevada, Utah, and Colorado. Settlers in the territory began pushing for statehood. This reignited bitter arguments about the spread of slavery. Which states should be free? Which should be slave states? The controversy threatened to rip apart the nation.

A Tougher Law

As in 1820, Congress worked out a compromise between the two factions, hoping to avert war. The section that caused the most controversy focused on fugitive slave laws. This time Congress passed legislation that strongly favored slave owners. The new laws required all citizens to help recover fugitive slaves. Those convicted of helping fugitives faced a steep fine of one thousand dollars and six months in jail. The new law abolished jury trials for fugitive slaves and put their fate into the hands of special commissioners. The commissioners received five dollars for each case they heard. If the fugitive was returned to the owner, the commissioner was awarded an additional five dollars. Slave owners did not have to produce warrants, and fugitives could be seized on only the word of a slaveholder. The law made it much easier for slaveholders to file claims for fugitive slaves. Congress also provided for many more federal officials to enforce the law.

The strict new law brought fresh terrors to the fugitive slaves who had escaped from the South. Under the law, fugitives who lived in the North as free blacks could be reclaimed by their former owners. The law made everyone in the United States legally responsible for finding and returning fugitive slaves. Even so, there were pockets of resistance among Northerners. Shortly after the passage of the law, abolitionists in Syracuse, New York, organized a mob to free a fugitive slave jailed in 1851. During a hearing on William Jerry Henry's case, abolitionists armed with clubs and axes beat down the door to the jail cell and freed the fugitive. Henry escaped to Canada.

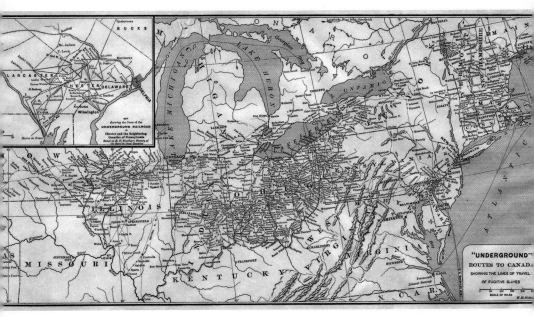

Map of the United States, showing in red the routes along the Underground Railroad which fugitives followed to freedom in the North and Canada

Other fugitives were not so lucky. In the first few months after the law was enacted, slaveholders tried to recapture more than one hundred fugitives in northern states. Those who did not escape were returned to the South and slavery or were killed during the attempt.

North of the North

Harriet Tubman joined many other fugitive slaves who fled to Canada after the Fugitive Slave Acts became law.

The Creation of Stark Mad Abolitionists

The recapture of Anthony Burns set the stage for the civil war that lay ahead and showed that fugitives would not be safe anywhere in the United States. Burns, a nineteen-year-old slave, escaped from a Virginia plantation in March of 1854. He settled in Boston, where he worked as a clerk in a clothing store. Boston, a hub of abolitionist activism, was home to William Lloyd Garrison and other noted abolitionists.

A poster proclaiming the kidnapping of Anthony Burns in Boston in 1854

Burns's former master, Charles Suttle, obtained a warrant for Burns's arrest. A deputy marshal seized Burns and locked him in a jail cell at the courthouse. Protesters stormed the courthouse and tried to rescue Burns, but armed deputies kept them at bay. During the brawl, a deputy was killed.

President Franklin Pierce called in the Marines, who circled the courthouse. As Burns was led away, fifty thousand protesters stood in the streets and jeered. Suttle later agreed to free Burns after being paid off by Boston supporters. But Boston residents did not forget or forgive. Mill owner Amos Lawrence wrote: "We went to bed one night old-fashioned, conservative, compromise, Union Whigs, and waked up stark mad Abolitionists."

A black woman who also fled to Canada after the law went into effect said she and her husband, a free black, "were comfortably settled in the States and were broken up by the Fugitive Slave Law—compelled to leave our home and friends, and to go at later than middle life into a foreign country among strangers." The First Report of the Anti-Slavery Society of Canada estimated that about thirty thousand blacks resided in Ontario (then known as Upper Canada) in 1852. Almost all the adults and many of the children had fled slavery in the United States.

A song popular among slaves of the time portrayed Canada as the Promised Land:

> I've served my master all my days
> Without a dime's reward,
> And now I'm forced to run away
> To flee the lash abhorred.
> The hounds are baying on my track—
> The master's just behind,
> Resolved that he will bring me back
> Before I cross the line.
> Farewell old master,
> Don't come after me,
> I'm on my way to Canada
> Where colored men are free.

Tubman settled in St. Catharines, Ontario. The enactment of the new fugitive slave law did not weaken her resolve to free the rest of her family from slavery. It merely lengthened her trip. Instead of Philadelphia, she now led fugitives into Canada.

Harriet Tubman, around 1895, when she was in her seventies. Tubman never lost a passenger on her many Underground Railroad trips.

The journey of more than 350 miles (563.3 km) took her through New York State and across Niagara Falls into Ottawa. In 1854, she arranged to meet her three brothers, Robert, Ben, and Henry, on Christmas Eve. To alert her brothers, she sent a coded letter to a free black friend, William Henry Jackson, who lived nearby and who could read and write. Authorities read the letter, but they did not understand its meaning. Jackson did and let Tubman's brothers know when she would arrive. The Brodesses planned to auction the brothers the day after Christmas.

On Christmas Eve, Ben and Henry met Tubman and together they set out for their father's property on the Thompson plantation. Ben's girlfriend, Jane, joined them. She wore a man's suit, which Ben had smuggled to her to disguise her appearance. Robert had stayed behind to assist his wife, who delivered the couple's third baby that day. Once the baby had been born, he raced for the meeting spot. Two other men arrived, and all seven spent Christmas Day huddled in the shed near the cabin. Their father brought them food and other supplies for their journey. They dared not let their mother know they were there or tell her of their plans. They feared she would give them away, crying and pleading for them not to go. From the shed, they watched Rit as she waited for her sons. She expected the brothers to come for Christmas dinner, but they never appeared.

At nightfall, the group headed north to freedom. They received food, clothing, and money for shoes from Thomas Garret when they reached his house in Wilmington, Delaware. Traveling one hundred miles over rough terrain "had worn their shoes off their feet," Tubman later told Sarah Bradford. Four days into their trip, they arrived at the Anti-Slavery Society Office, operated by William Still in Philadelphia. By then, two more fugitives had joined the band of freedom seekers. Following the Underground Railroad, the band headed for Western New York. They stopped at homes along the way and crossed the border into Canada.

Once there, the brothers adopted new names: Robert became John Stewart (or Seward), Ben became James Stewart (Seward), and Henry became William Henry Stewart (Seward). Jane became Catherine Stewart (Seward) when she married James. She said she had waited eight years to escape to Canada. John revealed that he had wanted to escape for the past twenty years.

CHAPTER FOUR

Freedom
at Last

After guiding her brothers to Canada, Harriet Tubman returned to Philadelphia to work and earn money for more trips to Maryland's Eastern Shore. With each journey she made south, she risked not only her freedom but also her life. As one of the few fugitive slaves returning to the South to lead people to freedom, Tubman had earned a reputation as the "Moses" of her people. In addition, she was among only a handful of women taking an active role in the Underground Railroad. In 1856, her name appeared in a book of narratives of fugitive slaves. In it, she said: "I have seen hundreds of escaped slaves, but I never saw one who was willing to go back and be a slave."

Members of the Sixth New York Artillery stand in the temporary kitchen area set up at a Union camp at Brandy Station, Virginia, during the Civil War.

Dangerous Rescues

During one of her treks leading slaves to freedom, Tubman waded across a river when she sensed danger on the road ahead. She urged the men with her to cross the swift, dark waters. When they refused, she walked across in water up to her chin. The men followed. Later they learned that officers were waiting on the road to capture them. By the time Tubman reached Delaware, she could barely talk. Besides having to travel in wet clothes, Tubman had been plagued by a toothache. With no other way to deal with the pain, she picked up a rock and knocked the tooth from her mouth.

On another trip, she led four slaves to freedom. Joe Bailey, who oversaw timber operations for a planter,

Harriet Tubman's longtime friend Thomas Garrett, a Quaker abolitionist and stationmaster, risked everything helping fugitives on the Underground Railroad.

asked Tubman to take him and three others to Canada. When the group arrived in Delaware, they learned that police stood along the bridge that led into Pennsylvania.

Tubman's friend Thomas Garrett hired a crew of black bricklayers to cross the bridge into Wilmington with a wagon loaded with supplies. The bricklayers greeted the officers as they passed. In the evening, the bricklayers returned, again exchanging greetings with police as they crossed into Pennsylvania. On the return trip, instead of supplies the wagon carried Tubman's group, hidden in a secret compartment covered with bricks.

After the group's narrow escape, Tubman became concerned about her parents. Both were technically free, but she feared that local officials would arrest her father for helping fugitives. Tubman returned to the Eastern Shore in the spring of 1857 to lead her parents—both in their seventies—to safety. They made their way to Canada, where they stayed with their sons.

During the next two years, Tubman advised freedom seekers about routes to follow to freedom. She also helped former slaves who had settled in St. Catharines. Several stayed in her home. Tubman became a popular speaker at antislavery gatherings and meetings pushing for women's rights.

Tubman's elderly parents did not like the cold Canadian winters. In 1859, William Seward offered to sell Tubman a small house and barn he owned just outside Auburn, New York. The price was low, $1,200, and Seward agreed to let her pay in installments. Tubman, along with her mother and father, moved into the house before the next winter.

In 1854, Congress had approved a new compromise allowing the territories of Kansas and Nebraska to choose for themselves whether to permit slavery within their borders. The deal repealed the earlier Missouri Compromise. This action led many to abandon hope that slavery would be ended through peaceful means. In 1859, John Brown led a small army of volunteers in an attack on the federal arsenal at Harpers Ferry, Virginia (later part of West Virginia). He hoped to spark a rebellion among slaves. Instead, his two sons

John Brown

and several others were killed. Brown was tried and hanged. Tubman had met the radical abolitionist in 1858 and helped him recruit former fugitives for his army. Brown referred to Tubman as the General and spoke highly of her leadership abilities. His death brought her great sorrow. The episode increased the friction between the South and the North.

In 1860, Tubman guided a family of five and two men to freedom. Pressure from slave owners and betrayals had compromised some of the stops along the Underground Railroad. Sometime during the journey, Tubman rapped out a special code on the door of a free black man who had sheltered her in the past. A white man stuck his head out an upstairs window and asked what she wanted. The black owner had been driven out of town because officials suspected he had helped runaway slaves. Tubman mumbled an excuse and quickly returned to the terrified fugitives. They hid in a nearby swamp. Soon a Quaker farmer walked by, talking loudly to himself about a wagon in a barnyard. Understanding the coded message, Tubman led her group to the man's farm, where they climbed aboard the wagon and rode to the next town. Somehow the farmer had heard of their dilemma and did what he could to help them.

The following year, on April 12, 1861, Southern rebels fired on Fort Sumter in the Charleston, South Carolina, harbor. Eleven states **seceded**, or separated, from the United States and set up their own nation: the **Confederate States of America**. After years of bitter disputes, the nation finally was at war.

Tubman: Soldier, Nurse, Cook, Spy

As the war raged, Tubman decided to help blacks living in Union (United States) Army camps in the South. Union soldiers overran the plantations, and slaves fled to the camps for protection. Massachusetts governor John Andrew, who met Tubman through abolitionist friends, arranged for her to travel to South Carolina.

Earlier Tubman had brought a young girl, Margaret Steward, to live with her. The mystery of this girl's relationship to Tubman has never been solved. Several researchers believe Margaret may have been Tubman's daughter. She left Margaret in the care of William Seward's sister-in-law. At age forty, Harriet Tubman headed for war.

Tubman arrived in Port Royal, South Carolina, in early 1862. Among other tasks, she organized a crew of black women who cooked and washed clothes for the soldiers. In addition, Tubman nursed soldiers felled by diseases such as malaria, pneumonia, and measles. She developed a reputation for herbal cures and treatments. Tubman also helped General David Hunter recruit soldiers for a black **regiment.** She received little pay for her work. To support herself, Tubman baked pies and made root beer, which she sold to Union soldiers.

For years, Tubman had eluded slave owners and made important connections among slaves, free blacks, and friendly white residents of Maryland. Making good use of those skills, she secretly met with slaves in South Carolina and gathered information about Confederate

Harriet Tubman, Expedition Leader

During the Civil War, Harriet Tubman worked closely with Colonel James Montgomery, a friend of John Brown. In June 1863, she learned where Confederates had stockpiled weapons and supplies and led Montgomery and his black regiments to the site. She was the first woman to plan and carry out such a mission during the Civil War.

Union troops destroyed nearby plantations, set fire to buildings, and loaded millions of dollars worth of supplies, cotton, and farm animals onto waiting gunboats.

They also signaled slaves in the area to flee the plantations. Upon hearing a whistle blow, hundreds of slaves—warned earlier by Tubman and her spies—ran to the shore. Carrying children, animals, and all their belongings, the slaves nearly swamped the boats. Tubman later likened the chaotic scene to the Bible's description of "the children of Israel, coming out of Egypt." Singing a hymn, she calmed the crowd as soldiers gradually evacuated them. They eventually transported more than seven hundred black men, women, and children to army camps in the area. More than one hundred black men joined the Union forces.

troops. Soon she was leading a network of black spies deep into enemy territory.

The End of the War

In September 1862, President Abraham Lincoln announced he would issue an order freeing slaves in all Confederate states. The **Emancipation Proclamation** became effective January 1, 1863.

John Wilkes Booth takes aim at Abraham Lincoln as the president and First Lady Mary Todd Lincoln watch a play at Ford's Theater on April 14, 1865.

On April 9, 1865, the Civil War ended when Confederate general Robert E. Lee surrendered at Appomattox Court House in Virginia. Within a week, President Lincoln died from an assassin's bullet. Seward, Tubman's friend and patron, almost lost his life, too. An associate of John Wilkes Booth, Lincoln's killer, stabbed Seward in the neck and throat the same night Lincoln was shot. The Secretary of State survived the attack, but he never fully recovered.

The nation, under the leadership of President Andrew Johnson, struggled to address the issues that continued to divide its people. While the Emancipation Proclamation ended slavery in the eleven Confederate states, it did not free slaves in states that had not seceded. The Thirteenth Amendment to the Constitution—which Congress passed in January 1865 and was ratified on December 6, 1865—abolished slavery throughout the United States and its territories.

For several months after the war, Tubman remained in Virginia nursing wounded soldiers. She headed home to Auburn in October. Riding the train from Philadelphia to New York, Tubman was told she had to ride in the baggage car. When she refused to budge, the conductor and two other men grabbed her and broke her arm. They threw her into the baggage car, where she lay—with injured arm and bruised ribs—until reaching New York. That was her homecoming from the war. Her friends in Auburn urged her to sue the railroad, but the effort was eventually dropped.

After the Underground

Despite her great contributions, Tubman never received a regular salary for her wartime duties. For years she tried without success to get the pension paid to other Civil War soldiers and nurses. Even with little money, she opened her home to former slaves. Several of her abolitionist friends, including the Sewards, donated funds to help with expenses.

In September 1867, a white man shot and killed Tubman's husband, John, in a dispute near his home in Maryland. The all-white jury found the man not guilty after discussing the case for ten minutes.

During that winter, Tubman organized efforts to raise money for **freedmen**—former slaves—in the South. Meanwhile, she continued to struggle to pay her own bills. Friends asked a local author, Sarah H. Bradford, to write Tubman's biography to raise money for her. *Scenes in the Life of Harriet Tubman* was released in 1869. A later edition, *Harriet Tubman, Moses of Her People*, followed

Photo of Harriet Tubman taken in 1911 when she was around ninety. She spent the last years of her life in Auburn, New York, and died in the home she founded for poor and elderly African Americans.

in 1886. The books helped pay her living expenses. Both books, though not completely accurate, also made Tubman famous. She became known as the "Black Joan of Arc." Queen Victoria of England showed her respect by sending Tubman a silver medal and a lace shawl.

In 1869, Tubman married a black Civil War veteran named Nelson Davis. A former slave, Davis had met Tubman when he boarded in her Auburn home. After their marriage, they operated a small farm

In 1908, the Harriet Tubman Home opened its doors to poor and elderly African Americans. The structure, pictured here, was restored by the AME Zion Church and reopened in 1953 as a tribute to Tubman's life and work.

and ran a brickmaking business in Auburn. The couple adopted a baby girl, Gertie, in 1874. Davis, who suffered from tuberculosis, died in 1888.

Tubman spent the last years of her life working to establish a home for poor and elderly black people. The Harriet Tubman Home for Aged and Indigent Negroes, later run by Tubman's church, served many needy black residents. She died there in 1913 of pneumonia.

In 1895 the government began paying Tubman a pension of eight dollars a month—not for her war service but as the widow of a black soldier. With the help of US

Representative Sereno Payne from New York, Tubman finally received a larger pension of twenty dollars a month, based on her service as a nurse during the war.

Sometime during the 1890s, the pain from Tubman's head injury became too much for her to bear. Surgeons at Massachusetts General Hospital operated on her brain and eased the pain. According to her obituary, Tubman refused to use anesthesia during the surgery. Instead, she bit on a bullet, just as the Civil War soldiers she tended had.

During her later years, Tubman continued to work for equal rights for blacks and women. She stirred audiences with tales of her success in her most famous role: conductor of the Underground Railroad. Her words still have the power to inspire:

> I was the conductor on the Underground Railroad for eight years, and I can say what most conductors can't say—I never ran my train off the track and I never lost a passenger.

Chronology

Dates in green pertain to events discussed in this volume.

1619 The African slave trade begins in North America.

1789 US Constitution goes into effect.

1777–1804 Slavery is abolished in the Northern states.

1808 The foreign slave trade is abolished by Great Britain and the United States.

circa 1822 Harriet Tubman is born into slavery in Dorchester County, Maryland.

1833 American Anti-Slavery Society is founded in Philadelphia.

ca. 1834–1836 Harriet Tubman defies a slave overseer and is struck in the head, a blow that leaves her with injuries to her brain. As a result, she has spells in which she suddenly falls asleep, sees visions, has seizures, and experiences vivid dreams.

1837–1839 The Grimké sisters speak against slavery to overflow audiences in New York and New England.

1844 Harriet Tubman marries John Tubman, a slave in Maryland.

1849 Harriet Tubman escapes from slavery into Pennsylvania.

1850 US Congress passes the Fugitive Slave Acts.

1851 *Uncle Tom's Cabin* runs as a serial in the abolitionist newspaper National Era in Washington, DC.

1851–1852 Harriet Tubman leads her brother Moses and several others to freedom in Pennsylvania.

1852 Stowe's complete novel, *Uncle Tom's Cabin*, sells millions of copies.

1854 Congress approves the Kansas-Nebraska Act. Harriet Tubman guides her three brothers, Ben, Robert, and Henry, and several others from the Eastern Shore of Maryland to safety in Canada.

1855–1860 Harriet Tubman rescues freedom seekers and leads them from Maryland to Canada. In all, she makes about thirteen trips and escorts about seventy enslaved people to freedom.

1857 Harriet Tubman leads her parents out of Maryland and settles them in Canada.

1856 Proslavery activists attack the antislavery town of Lawrence, Kansas; John Brown leads a raid on a proslavery family, which launches a three-month conflict known as "Bleeding Kansas."

1857 Supreme Court hands down decision in the *Dred Scott v. Sanford* case.

1859 John Brown launches an attack at Harpers Ferry. He is captured, tried, and executed. Harriet Tubman is one of his advisors.

1860 Abraham Lincoln is elected president; South Carolina secedes from the Union. Harriet Tubman speaks at a women's suffrage meeting in Boston. She continues her support for the women's rights movement throughout her life and attends meetings into the early 1900s.

1861 Civil War begins.

1862 Harriet Tubman sails to Beaufort, South Carolina, and begins service as a nurse at a US army hospital located there.

1863 Lincoln's Emancipation Proclamation frees the slaves in Confederate-held territory; Harriet Tubman joins the Union regiment led by Colonel James Montgomery, scouts behind the lines, and leads an expedition that rescues more than seven hundred slaves.

1865 The Civil War ends. President Lincoln is assassinated. The Thirteenth Amendment to the US Constitution abolishes slavery.

1866 The American Equal Rights Association is formed. Its goals are to establish equal rights and the vote for women and African Americans.

1868 Fourteenth Amendment grants US citizenship to former slaves.

1869 Harriet Tubman marries Nelson Davis, a veteran of the Union Army.

1870 Fifteenth Amendment gives black men the right to vote.

1896 A group of black civil rights activists form the National Association of Colored Women in Washington, DC. The group works to further civil rights for blacks and obtain the vote for women.

1913 Harriet Tubman dies of pneumonia at the home for aged blacks she founded in Auburn, New York.

1990 President George H. W. Bush declares March 10 as Harriet Tubman Day.

Glossary

abolitionist movement The campaign to ban slavery in the United States.

agent People who provided information and helped runaway slaves in other ways.

conductor A person, such as Harriet Tubman, who led slaves out of the South to freedom along the Underground Railroad.

Confederate States of America The government formed by the eleven Southern states that withdrew from the United States during the Civil War.

Emancipation Proclamation President Abraham Lincoln's order, in 1863, to free the slaves in the eleven states of the Confederacy.

free states States that banned slavery within their borders.

freedmen Freed slaves.

freedom seeker One who flees slavery; also called a fugitive or a runaway.

lynch To murder, usually by hanging, by a mob.

master A white slave owner.

plantation Large farms in the South where cotton, rice, tobacco, or other crops were grown.

regiment A unit of soldiers under the command of an officer.

secede To withdraw from. The Southern states seceded from the United States during the Civil War.

slave catchers People paid to recapture runaway slaves.

slave state A state that allowed slavery within its borders.

slave trade The business of capturing and transporting slaves to be sold in South, Central, and North America.

stationmasters People who ran stations.

stations Safe houses or places where runaway slaves could hide and rest.

Underground Railroad The secret network of escape routes and safe houses leading from the South to freedom in Mexico, the northern United States, and later, Canada.

Union The states remaining as part of the United States during the Civil War.

Further Information

Books

Adler, David A. *Harriet Tubman and the Underground Railroad*. New York: Holiday House, 2012.

Calkhoven, Laurie. *Harriet Tubman: Leading the Way to Freedom*. New York: Sterling Publishing, 2008.

Gold, Susan Dudley. *Missouri Compromise*. Landmark Legislation. New York: Marshall Cavendish Benchmark, 2011.

McDonough, Yona Zeldis. *What Was the Underground Railroad?* New York: Grosset & Dunlap, 2013.

Sawyer, Kem Knapp. *Harriet Tubman*. DK Biography. New York: DK Children, 2010.

Websites

Born in Slavery: Slave Narratives from the Federal Writers' Project, 1936–1938

memory.loc.gov/ammem/snhtml/snhome.html

Explore more than 2,300 first-person accounts of slavery and 500 black-and-white photographs of former slaves—all collected during the 1930s.

Harriet Tubman Special Resource Study

parkplanning.nps.gov/projectHome.cfm?projectID=11008

Read the biography of Harriet Tubman's life. Learn more about the research being done on her participation in the Civil War.

Harriet Tubman Visitor Center

www.harriettubman.com

View historical documents and photos, and take a virtual tour of the freedom trail followed by Harriet Tubman.

National Underground Railroad Freedom Center

www.freedomcenter.org

Learn more about slavery worldwide, past and present. Explore the section on the Underground Railroad.

Bibliography

BlackPast.org. "Remembered & Reclaimed." Accessed December 20, 2014. www.blackpast.org.

Bordewich, Fergus M. *Bound for Canaan: The Underground Railroad and the War for the Soul of America.* New York: HarperCollins Publishers, 2005.

Bradford, Sarah. *Harriet: The Moses of Her People.* New York: Geo R. Lockwood & Son, 1886.

———. *Scenes in the Life of Harriet Tubman.* Auburn, NY: W. J. Moses, Printer, 1869.

Brawley, Benjamin Griffith. "Women of Achievement: 1882–1939." Accessed December 20, 2014. http://docsouth.unc.edu/church/brawley/brawley.html#ill2.

Calarco, Tom. "The Remarkable Story of Peter Still, William Still, and Seth Concklin." Accessed December 20, 2014. www.undergroundrailroadconductor.com/Still-Concklin.htm.

Clinton, Catherine. *Harriet Tubman: The Road to Freedom.* New York: Little, Brown and Company, 2004.

Collison, Gary L. *Shadrach Minkins: From Fugitive Slave to Citizen.* Boston: Harvard University Press, 1998.

Einhorn, Robin L. *American Taxation, American Slavery.* Chicago: University of Chicago Press, 2008.

Harper, Douglas. "Slavery in the North." Accessed December 20, 2014. www.slavenorth.com.

Kohn, Martin. "South to Freedom." *Humanities* 34, no. 2 (March/April 2013).

Larson, Kate Clifford. *Bound for the Promised Land: Harriet Tubman: Portrait of an American Hero*. New York: Ballantine Books, 2004.

———. "Harriet Tubman Myths and Facts." Accessed December 20, 2014. www.harriettubmanbiography.com/harriet-tubman-myths-and-facts.html.

Library of Congress. "Our Documents." Accessed December 20, 2014. www.ourdocuments.gov.

National Park Service. "Network to Freedom." Accessed December 20, 2014. www.nps.gov/subjects/ugrr/index.htm.

PBS. "Africans in America." Accessed December 20, 2014. www.pbs.org/wgbh/aia/home.html.

Siebert, Wilbur. *The Underground Railroad in Massachusetts*. Worcester, MA: American Antiquarian Society, 1936.

WNET. "African American Migrations, 1600s to Present: The African Americans: Many Rivers to Cross." Accessed December 20, 2014. www.pbs.org/wnet/african-americans-many-rivers-to-cross/history/on-african-american-migrations.

Index

About the Author

SUSAN DUDLEY GOLD is a writer, historian, editor, and graphic designer. She worked as a newspaper reporter and magazine editor before becoming a children's book author. She has written more than fifty books for middle- and high-school students on a wide range of topics. Her book on slavery and human rights, *United States v. Amistad: Slave Ship Mutiny* (Supreme Court Milestones), received a Carter G. Woodson Honor Book award. She has also written about slavery and civil rights in *Missouri Compromise* (Landmark Legislation), *Civil Rights Act of 1964* (Landmark Legislation), and *Brown v. Board of Education: Separate but Equal?* (Supreme Court Milestones). After serving a year as a VISTA volunteer, she currently manages a program to aid veterans. Gold and her husband live in Maine, where the couple owns a web design and publishing company.